Timeless Grandma Old Fashion Cookbook
Heirloom Flavors from the Hearth of the Kitchen

JUSTIN S. LEE

All rights reserved.No part of this publication may be reproduced, distributed, or transmitted in any form or by any means, including photocopying, recording, or other electronic or mechanical methods, without the prior written permission of the publisher, except in the case of brief quotations embodied in critical reviews and certain other noncommercial uses permitted by copyright law.

Copyright © JUSTIN S. LEE 2025

Introduction

There is something truly magical about stepping into Grandma's kitchen. It's more than just a place where meals are prepared—it's a sanctuary of memories, a haven filled with the aroma of freshly baked bread, the comforting warmth of a simmering stew, and the gentle hum of stories passed down through generations. This cookbook, *Timeless Grandma Old Fashion Cookbook: Heirloom Flavors from the Heart of the Kitchen*, is an invitation to take that journey back to a time when cooking was slow, deliberate, and wrapped in love.

In today's fast-paced world, convenience often takes center stage. Ready-made meals, quick fixes, and instant recipes flood our lives, promising efficiency but sometimes at the cost of connection and flavor. Yet, there is an undeniable charm and satisfaction in the old-fashioned way of cooking—where each ingredient is chosen with care, each dish is crafted by hand, and every meal tells a story. Grandma's kitchen was the heart of the home, a place where love was measured in spoonfuls of sugar, patience was the secret seasoning, and every bite was a comforting reminder of family and tradition.

This book is not just a collection of recipes. It is a celebration of heritage and the simple joys found in timeless cooking. It captures the essence of those heirloom flavors that have stood the test of time, recipes that have been lovingly perfected and passed down, sometimes scribbled on worn recipe cards or shared quietly during a lazy afternoon in the kitchen. These dishes bring together the past and the present, offering more than nourishment—they offer a connection to the people who cooked them and the lives they touched.

When you flip through these pages, you will find breakfasts that start the day with warmth and comfort, soups and stews that wrap you in a cozy embrace, breads that fill the air with irresistible aroma, and desserts that sweeten not only the palate but also the soul. Every recipe has been selected to honor the spirit of home cooking—simple ingredients, straightforward methods, and that extra pinch of love that only Grandma knew how to add.

What makes old-fashioned cooking special isn't just the recipes themselves, but the way they bring people together. In Grandma's kitchen, meals were never just about eating—they were about sharing moments, laughter, and stories. It was where family gathered after long days, where neighbors were welcomed with open arms, and where the art of hospitality was practiced effortlessly. This book encourages you to recreate that feeling in your own kitchen—to slow down, savor the process, and make food that's not just good but meaningful.

You might wonder why these old recipes still matter today. The answer lies in their simplicity and their soul. They remind us that good food doesn't need to be complicated or expensive; it just needs to be made with care. They also remind us of resilience—of how families have relied on what was available, creating nourishing meals out of humble ingredients, transforming leftovers into treasures, and turning celebrations into lifelong memories.

In these pages, you'll find practical advice as well—kitchen tips and tricks that Grandma swore by, ways to preserve the harvest with preserves and pickles, and suggestions for making your cooking more intentional and connected. This is about more than following instructions; it's about embracing a mindset, a way of living that honors the past while feeding the future.

This cookbook is for anyone who longs for the taste of tradition, whether you grew up with a grandmother who cooked or are discovering these flavors anew. It's for those who want to create meals that comfort and nourish, who value the stories food can tell, and who believe that the heart of a home is found in its kitchen.

So, take a moment to breathe in the warmth, roll up your sleeves, and step into a kitchen filled with timeless aromas and treasured memories. Let this book be your guide to heirloom flavors, and may every recipe you try become part of your family's story—just as they were part of Grandma's.

Welcome to a journey of flavor, history, and love. Welcome to Grandma's kitchen.

Chapter 1: Breakfast Classics to Start Your Day

Breakfast has always held a special place in Grandma's kitchen. It was the meal that gathered the family around the table, promising a fresh start filled with warmth and comfort. Long before the rush of modern life, breakfasts were slow and meaningful—fluffy pancakes stacked high, biscuits fresh from the oven, and eggs cooked just the way everyone liked them. These dishes weren't just about filling hungry bellies; they were about beginning the day with love and tradition.

In this chapter, you'll discover recipes that bring those old-fashioned mornings back to life. From sweet to savory, each recipe carries the aroma of a simpler time when the kitchen was the heart of the home and breakfast was a cherished ritual.

Grandma's Fluffy Pancakes and Syrups

There's nothing quite like the sight of a stack of golden, fluffy pancakes on a Sunday morning. Grandma's pancakes were always light and airy, made from simple ingredients and cooked on a well-seasoned griddle. The secret was in the balance—just enough baking powder for lift and a touch of buttermilk for tang and tenderness.

To accompany these pancakes, Grandma had a variety of homemade syrups: from rich maple syrup to fruity berry compotes and even a sweet cinnamon butter that melted slowly over the warm stack. These syrups weren't just toppings—they were part of the experience, made with fresh, natural ingredients and the same care as the pancakes themselves.

The Perfect Southern Biscuits and Gravy

Biscuits and gravy are a Southern classic that brings comfort like no other. Grandma's biscuits were flaky and tender, made from scratch using real buttermilk and a careful hand to ensure they rose just right. The gravy, made from savory sausage and creamy milk, was seasoned with cracked black pepper and a pinch of love.

This dish was a staple for weekend breakfasts, served hot and hearty to fuel the family for the day ahead. The key is patience in mixing and baking—rushing the dough or overworking it can rob the biscuits of their delicate layers. When done right, biscuits and gravy turn a simple meal into a soul-soothing tradition.

Hearty Oatmeal and Warm Porridge Recipes

Before the rise of quick cereals and instant oatmeal packets, porridge was the breakfast of choice. Grandma's oatmeal was slow-cooked to creamy perfection, often enhanced with cinnamon sticks, a splash of cream, and a drizzle of honey or molasses.

Porridge was a humble dish but packed with nutrition and comfort. It was often served with dried fruits or nuts, making it both wholesome and satisfying. This section includes tips for cooking perfect oatmeal and variations to suit different tastes, ensuring a warm, hearty start even on the coldest mornings.

Traditional Egg Dishes with a Twist

Eggs were never boring in Grandma's kitchen. Whether fried, scrambled, or baked into casseroles, eggs formed the centerpiece of many breakfasts. Grandma's secret was in simple additions—fresh herbs from the garden, a sprinkle of sharp cheese, or a dash of pepper and paprika.

You'll find recipes for classic scrambled eggs with herbs, baked egg casseroles perfect for feeding a crowd, and even old-fashioned deviled eggs that made their way from breakfast to parties. These dishes remind us that eggs are versatile, nourishing, and endlessly adaptable to the tastes and traditions of each family.

Chapter 2: Soups & Stews — Detailed Recipes and Instructions

Grandma's Chicken and Dumplings

Ingredients:

- 1 whole chicken (about 4 pounds), cut into pieces
- 8 cups water
- 3 celery stalks, chopped
- 2 large carrots, peeled and chopped
- 1 large onion, quartered
- 2 bay leaves
- 1 teaspoon salt (adjust to taste)

- 1/2 teaspoon black pepper
- 2 cups all-purpose flour
- 1 tablespoon baking powder
- 1 teaspoon salt
- 1 cup buttermilk
- 3 tablespoons melted butter or vegetable oil
- Fresh parsley, chopped (optional, for garnish)

Cooking Time:

- Stock simmering: 1.5 to 2 hours
- Dumpling cooking: 20 minutes

Cooking Tips:

- Use a heavy-bottomed pot to simmer the stock evenly.

- Skim off any foam or impurities that rise to the top during simmering for a clearer broth.

- Don't overmix the dumpling batter; gently fold ingredients to keep them light and fluffy.

- Drop dumplings carefully into simmering broth and avoid stirring once added to prevent them from breaking apart.

Instructions:

1. **Make the chicken stock:** Place the chicken pieces in a large pot with water, celery, carrots, onion, bay leaves, salt, and pepper. Bring to a boil over medium-high heat. Reduce to low and let it simmer gently for 1.5 to 2 hours, uncovered. Occasionally skim the surface to remove foam.

2. **Remove chicken:** After simmering, carefully remove the chicken pieces and set aside to cool. Strain the broth through a fine sieve or cheesecloth into another pot to remove vegetables and bay leaves.

3. **Prepare dumpling batter:** In a mixing bowl, combine the flour, baking powder, and salt. Stir in the buttermilk and melted butter until just combined. The batter should be thick but sticky.

4. **Shred chicken:** Once the chicken is cool enough to handle, remove the meat from the bones and shred into bite-sized pieces. Discard bones and skin.

5. **Cook dumplings:** Bring the strained broth back to a gentle simmer. Drop spoonfuls of dumpling batter into the simmering broth, spacing them evenly. Cover and cook for 15-20 minutes without lifting the lid. Dumplings will puff up and cook through.

6. **Combine and serve:** Add shredded chicken back into the pot during the last 5 minutes to warm through. Taste and adjust seasoning as needed. Garnish with fresh parsley if desired. Serve hot.

Hearty Beef Stew with Root Vegetables

Ingredients:

- 2 pounds beef chuck, cut into 1-inch cubes

- Salt and freshly ground black pepper

- 3 tablespoons all-purpose flour

- 3 tablespoons vegetable oil or bacon fat
- 1 large onion, chopped
- 3 garlic cloves, minced
- 4 cups beef broth or stock
- 2 cups water
- 4 large carrots, peeled and cut into chunks
- 3 medium potatoes, peeled and cubed
- 2 parsnips, peeled and sliced
- 2 turnips, peeled and cubed (optional)
- 2 teaspoons dried thyme or 4 sprigs fresh thyme
- 2 bay leaves
- 1 tablespoon tomato paste (optional)
- Fresh parsley for garnish

Cooking Time:

- Prep and browning: 30 minutes

- Simmering: 2.5 to 3 hours

Cooking Tips:

- Pat meat dry before dredging in flour to achieve a good sear.

- Brown meat in batches to avoid overcrowding the pan.

- Use a heavy pot with a tight-fitting lid for even heat retention.

- Add vegetables according to their cooking times; root vegetables can be added all at once but keep an eye to avoid overcooking.

- For a thicker stew, mash some of the potatoes in the pot towards the end of cooking.

Instructions:

1. **Prepare the beef:** Season beef cubes generously with salt and pepper. Dredge in flour, shaking off any excess.

2. **Brown the beef:** Heat oil or bacon fat in a large Dutch oven or heavy pot over medium-high heat. Brown beef cubes in batches until deeply caramelized on all sides. Remove browned beef and set aside.

3. **Sauté aromatics:** In the same pot, add chopped onion and sauté until softened, about 5 minutes. Add garlic and cook for another minute. Stir in tomato paste if using, cooking for 1-2 minutes to develop flavor.

4. **Deglaze and simmer:** Pour in beef broth and water, scraping up any browned bits from the bottom of the pot. Return beef to the pot. Add thyme, bay leaves, and more salt and pepper if needed. Bring to a simmer.

5. **Cook stew:** Cover and reduce heat to low. Let the stew simmer gently for 2 hours, stirring occasionally.

6. **Add vegetables:** Add carrots, potatoes, parsnips, and turnips to the pot. Continue simmering, covered, for another 1 to 1.5 hours, until vegetables and beef are tender.

7. **Final seasoning:** Remove bay leaves and thyme sprigs. Taste and adjust seasoning. If you want a thicker broth, mash some potatoes against the side of the pot and stir.

8. **Serve:** Ladle stew into bowls, garnish with fresh parsley, and serve with crusty bread.

Classic Creamy Corn Chowder

Ingredients:

- 4 cups fresh or frozen corn kernels
- 3 medium potatoes, peeled and diced
- 1 medium onion, diced
- 2 celery stalks, diced
- 3 tablespoons butter
- 3 tablespoons all-purpose flour
- 4 cups chicken or vegetable broth
- 1 cup milk or cream

- Salt and pepper to taste
- 1 teaspoon dried thyme (optional)
- Chopped chives or parsley for garnish

Cooking Time:

- Prep and sautéing: 15 minutes
- Simmering: 30 minutes

Cooking Tips:

- Fresh corn is best when in season, but frozen works well year-round.
- For extra flavor, save some corn kernels to add raw near the end of cooking for a bit of crunch.
- Don't boil after adding milk or cream to prevent curdling; heat gently instead.
- Stir frequently when thickening with flour to avoid lumps.

Instructions:

1. **Sauté vegetables:** In a large pot, melt butter over medium heat. Add onion and celery, cooking until softened, about 5 minutes.

2. **Make roux:** Sprinkle flour over vegetables and stir well to coat. Cook for 2 minutes to remove raw flour taste, stirring constantly.

3. **Add liquids:** Gradually whisk in broth, ensuring no lumps form. Bring to a simmer.

4. **Cook potatoes and corn:** Add diced potatoes and corn kernels (reserve a handful if you want crunchy kernels later). Simmer until potatoes are tender, about 20 minutes.

5. **Add milk and season:** Stir in milk or cream gently, warm through without boiling. Add thyme if using. Season with salt and pepper to taste.

6. **Finish and serve:** If using reserved corn kernels, stir them in now and cook 2-3 minutes. Garnish with chives or parsley. Serve with warm bread.

Old-Fashioned Lentil and Vegetable Soup

Ingredients:

- 1 1/2 cups dried lentils, rinsed and sorted
- 1 large onion, diced
- 2 carrots, diced
- 2 celery stalks, diced
- 3 garlic cloves, minced
- 4 cups vegetable or chicken broth
- 2 cups water
- 1 cup diced tomatoes (canned or fresh)
- 2 teaspoons dried thyme or 3 sprigs fresh thyme
- 4 ounces bacon or ham (optional), diced

- 2 tablespoons olive oil or bacon fat
- Salt and pepper to taste
- Fresh parsley for garnish

Cooking Time:

- Prep and sauté: 15 minutes
- Simmering: 45 minutes to 1 hour

Cooking Tips:

- Rinse lentils thoroughly to remove debris.
- Lentils do not require soaking, but rinsing helps.
- Use bacon or ham for a smoky depth, or omit for vegetarian version.
- Adjust thickness by adding more broth or water as needed.
- For a creamier texture, puree part of the soup with a blender before serving.

Instructions:

1. **Prepare the base:** Heat olive oil or bacon fat in a large pot over medium heat. Add bacon or ham if using, cook until browned and crisp. Remove and set aside, leaving fat in the pot.

2. **Sauté vegetables:** Add onion, carrots, celery, and garlic to the pot. Cook until softened, about 7-10 minutes.

3. **Add lentils and liquids:** Stir in lentils, broth, water, tomatoes, and thyme. Bring to a boil, then reduce to a gentle simmer.

4. **Cook the soup:** Cover partially and simmer for 45 minutes to 1 hour, until lentils are tender and soup thickens. Stir occasionally.

5. **Finish seasoning:** Return cooked bacon or ham to the pot. Season with salt and pepper to taste. If desired, blend part of the soup for creaminess.

6. **Serve:** Garnish with fresh parsley and serve with crusty bread or cornbread.

Each of these recipes invites you to slow down and savor the process of cooking, embracing the old-fashioned ways that turn simple ingredients into deeply satisfying meals. They are perfect for nourishing both body and soul, reflecting the love and care found in Grandma's.

Chapter 3: Breads & Baking — From Scratch Goodness

Baking bread and sweets from scratch has always been at the heart of Grandma's kitchen. The smell of freshly baked bread wafting through the house was a daily comfort, a signal of warmth, welcome, and care. From tender biscuits to sweet cinnamon rolls, these recipes represent the joy of creating something delicious and timeless with simple ingredients and a bit of patience.

In this chapter, you will find detailed recipes for the classic breads and baked goods that every family treasured—each one made the old-fashioned way, with techniques and tips passed down through generations. Baking from scratch might take time, but the results are incredibly rewarding: warm, flaky, and flavorful creations that bring people together.

Grandma's Famous Homemade Bread

Ingredients:

- 4 cups all-purpose flour (plus extra for kneading)

- 1 packet (2 1/4 teaspoons) active dry yeast
- 1 1/2 teaspoons salt
- 1 1/2 cups warm water (110°F/43°C)
- 2 tablespoons sugar
- 2 tablespoons melted butter or vegetable oil

Cooking Time:

- Preparation and rising: 2 to 2.5 hours
- Baking: 30 to 35 minutes

Cooking Tips:

- Use warm water to activate the yeast but avoid temperatures over 120°F to prevent killing it.
- Allow the dough to rise in a warm, draft-free place for the best results.

- Knead the dough until it's smooth and elastic, about 8-10 minutes by hand.

- Don't rush the rising process; good bread needs time to develop flavor and texture.

Instructions:

1. **Activate yeast:** In a small bowl, dissolve sugar in warm water. Sprinkle yeast over the top and let it sit for 5-10 minutes until foamy.

2. **Mix dough:** In a large bowl, combine flour and salt. Add the yeast mixture and melted butter. Stir until a shaggy dough forms.

3. **Knead:** Turn dough onto a floured surface. Knead for 8-10 minutes until smooth and elastic.

4. **First rise:** Place dough in a greased bowl, cover with a clean towel, and let it rise in a warm spot until doubled in size, about 1 to 1.5 hours.

5. **Shape:** Punch down dough, shape into a loaf, and place in a greased loaf pan or on a baking sheet. Cover and let rise again until doubled, about 45 minutes.

6. **Bake:** Preheat oven to 375°F (190°C). Bake for 30-35 minutes until golden brown and hollow-sounding when tapped.

7. **Cool:** Remove from pan and cool on a rack before slicing.

Sweet Cinnamon Rolls and Sticky Buns

Ingredients for Dough:

- 4 cups all-purpose flour
- 1 packet active dry yeast
- 1 cup warm milk (110°F)
- 1/3 cup sugar
- 1/3 cup melted butter
- 1 teaspoon salt
- 2 eggs

Filling:

- 1 cup brown sugar
- 2 tablespoons cinnamon
- 1/2 cup softened butter

Glaze:

- 1 cup powdered sugar
- 2 tablespoons milk
- 1/2 teaspoon vanilla extract

Cooking Time:

- Dough rising: 1.5 to 2 hours
- Baking: 25 to 30 minutes

Cooking Tips:

- Keep dough moist but not sticky; adjust flour if necessary.
- Roll dough evenly for uniform rolls.
- Let rolls rise fully before baking for a fluffy texture.
- Brush rolls with melted butter before adding filling for extra richness.

Instructions:

1. **Prepare dough:** Dissolve yeast in warm milk with a pinch of sugar. In a large bowl, combine flour, sugar, salt, melted butter, eggs, and yeast mixture. Mix into a soft dough.

2. **Knead and rise:** Knead dough on a floured surface for 8-10 minutes. Place in greased bowl, cover, and let rise until doubled, about 1 to 1.5 hours.

3. **Roll and fill:** Roll dough into a rectangle about 16x12 inches. Spread softened butter over dough, sprinkle with cinnamon and brown sugar evenly.

4. **Form rolls:** Roll dough tightly from the long edge. Cut into 12 equal pieces and place in greased baking pan.

5. **Second rise:** Cover and let rise 30-45 minutes.

6. **Bake:** Preheat oven to 350°F (175°C). Bake rolls for 25-30 minutes until golden brown.

7. **Glaze:** Mix powdered sugar, milk, and vanilla to a smooth glaze. Drizzle over warm rolls before serving.

Buttermilk Cornbread, Perfect Every Time

Ingredients:

- 1 cup cornmeal
- 1 cup all-purpose flour
- 1/4 cup sugar
- 1 teaspoon baking powder
- 1/2 teaspoon baking soda
- 1/2 teaspoon salt

- 1 1/4 cups buttermilk
- 1/4 cup melted butter
- 2 large eggs

Cooking Time:

- Prep: 10 minutes
- Bake: 20 to 25 minutes

Cooking Tips:

- Use fresh buttermilk for tangy flavor and tender crumb.
- Don't overmix; stir ingredients until just combined.
- Bake in a preheated cast-iron skillet for a crispy crust.

Instructions:

1. **Preheat oven:** to 400°F (200°C). Grease a 9-inch cast-iron skillet or baking pan.

2. **Mix dry ingredients:** In a bowl, whisk cornmeal, flour, sugar, baking powder, baking soda, and salt.

3. **Combine wet ingredients:** In another bowl, whisk buttermilk, melted butter, and eggs.

4. **Mix batter:** Pour wet ingredients into dry and stir until just combined.

5. **Bake:** Pour batter into skillet and bake 20-25 minutes until golden and a toothpick inserted comes out clean.

6. **Cool and serve:** Let cool slightly before slicing. Serve warm with butter or honey.

Old-Fashioned Pie Crust and Fruit Pies

Ingredients for Pie Crust:

- 2 1/2 cups all-purpose flour
- 1 teaspoon salt
- 1 cup (2 sticks) cold unsalted butter, cubed

- 6-8 tablespoons ice water

Ingredients for Filling (Classic Apple Pie):

- 6 cups peeled and sliced tart apples (such as Granny Smith)
- 3/4 cup sugar
- 2 tablespoons all-purpose flour
- 1 teaspoon cinnamon
- 1/4 teaspoon nutmeg
- 1 tablespoon lemon juice

Cooking Time:

- Pie crust prep: 20-30 minutes
- Baking: 45-55 minutes

Cooking Tips:

- Keep butter and water cold to ensure flaky crust.

- Use a pastry cutter or food processor for cutting butter into flour.

- Don't overwork dough to avoid tough crust.

- Chill dough before rolling.

Instructions:

1. **Make crust:** Combine flour and salt in a bowl. Cut in cold butter until mixture resembles coarse crumbs. Slowly add ice water, one tablespoon at a time, until dough comes together. Divide dough into two disks and chill 30 minutes.

2. **Prepare filling:** Toss apples with sugar, flour, cinnamon, nutmeg, and lemon juice.

3. **Roll out dough:** Roll one disk into a 12-inch circle and fit into 9-inch pie pan.

4. **Add filling:** Pour apple mixture into crust.

5. **Top crust:** Roll out second disk and place over filling. Trim and crimp edges. Cut slits in top for steam to escape.

6. **Bake:** Preheat oven to 425°F (220°C). Bake 15 minutes, then reduce heat to 350°F (175°C) and bake 30-40 minutes more until crust is golden and filling bubbly.

7. **Cool:** Let cool before slicing.

Chapter 4: Main Dishes — Hearty & Soulful

Grandma's main dishes were always the heart of the family meal—recipes designed to satisfy, nourish, and bring everyone to the table. These meals combined simple, accessible ingredients with time-tested techniques to create flavors that are rich, comforting, and full of soul. From slow-cooked roasts to crispy fried chicken, these dishes embody the spirit of old-fashioned home cooking, where every bite tells a story of love and tradition.

In this chapter, you'll find detailed recipes that celebrate hearty, soulful cooking—meals that warmed the home and made gatherings memorable. Each recipe comes with tips to help you recreate these classics with confidence, even if you're new to traditional cooking.

Sunday Pot Roast with Pan Gravy

Ingredients:

- 3 to 4 pounds beef chuck roast

- Salt and freshly ground black pepper
- 3 tablespoons vegetable oil or bacon fat
- 1 large onion, sliced
- 4 cloves garlic, smashed
- 4 carrots, peeled and cut into chunks
- 4 celery stalks, cut into chunks
- 2 cups beef broth
- 1 cup red wine (optional)
- 2 sprigs fresh rosemary
- 2 sprigs fresh thyme
- 2 bay leaves

Cooking Time:

- Prep and browning: 30 minutes

- Braising: 3 to 4 hours

Cooking Tips:

- Choose a well-marbled chuck roast for tenderness.

- Brown the meat thoroughly for deep flavor.

- Use a heavy Dutch oven or oven-safe pot with a lid for even cooking.

- Low and slow braising breaks down tough connective tissue for melt-in-your-mouth results.

- Let roast rest before slicing to keep juices locked in.

Instructions:

1. **Preheat oven:** to 325°F (160°C).

2. **Season roast:** Generously season roast with salt and pepper on all sides.

3. **Brown roast:** Heat oil in Dutch oven over medium-high heat. Brown roast on all sides until deeply caramelized,

about 4-5 minutes per side. Remove and set aside.

4. **Sauté vegetables:** Add onions, garlic, carrots, and celery to pot. Cook until softened, about 5-7 minutes.

5. **Deglaze:** Pour in red wine (if using) and beef broth, scraping up browned bits from bottom of pot.

6. **Add herbs and roast:** Return roast to pot. Add rosemary, thyme, and bay leaves. Cover and place in oven.

7. **Braise:** Cook for 3 to 4 hours, turning roast halfway through, until meat is fork-tender.

8. **Rest and slice:** Remove roast and let rest for 15 minutes before slicing.

9. **Make pan gravy:** Strain cooking liquid into a saucepan. Skim off excess fat. Simmer until slightly thickened or whisk in a slurry of flour and water for thicker gravy. Season to taste.

10. **Serve:** Slice roast and serve with pan gravy and braised vegetables.

Classic Meatloaf with Secret Ingredients

Ingredients:

- 2 pounds ground beef
- 1 cup breadcrumbs
- 1/2 cup milk
- 2 eggs
- 1 small onion, finely chopped
- 2 cloves garlic, minced
- 1/2 cup ketchup (plus extra for topping)
- 2 tablespoons Worcestershire sauce
- 1 teaspoon salt
- 1/2 teaspoon black pepper

- 1 teaspoon dried thyme
- 1/4 cup grated Parmesan cheese (secret ingredient)

Cooking Time:

- Prep: 20 minutes
- Baking: 1 hour

Cooking Tips:

- Don't overmix meat to keep meatloaf tender.
- Use fresh breadcrumbs for better texture.
- Rest meatloaf after baking to hold shape when slicing.
- The Parmesan adds umami depth without overpowering.

Instructions:

1. **Preheat oven:** to 350°F (175°C).

2. **Mix ingredients:** In a large bowl, soak breadcrumbs in milk for 5 minutes. Add ground beef, eggs, onion, garlic, ketchup, Worcestershire sauce, salt, pepper, thyme, and Parmesan. Mix gently with hands until just combined.

3. **Shape loaf:** Form mixture into a loaf shape on a greased baking sheet or in a loaf pan.

4. **Top with ketchup:** Spread a thin layer of ketchup over the top.

5. **Bake:** Cook for about 1 hour, until internal temperature reaches 160°F (70°C).

6. **Rest:** Let meatloaf rest for 10 minutes before slicing.

7. **Serve:** Slice and serve with mashed potatoes or your favorite sides.

Fried Chicken the Way Grandma Made It

Ingredients:

- 4 pounds bone-in, skin-on chicken pieces (legs, thighs, breasts)
- 2 cups buttermilk
- 2 cups all-purpose flour
- 1 tablespoon paprika
- 1 teaspoon garlic powder
- 1 teaspoon onion powder
- 1 teaspoon salt
- 1/2 teaspoon black pepper
- Vegetable oil for frying

Cooking Time:

- Marinating: 4 hours to overnight
- Frying: 15 to 20 minutes

Cooking Tips:

- Marinate chicken in buttermilk overnight for tender, flavorful meat.

- Use a heavy-bottomed skillet or cast-iron pan for even frying.

- Maintain oil temperature between 325°F and 350°F for crispy crust without greasiness.

- Don't overcrowd pan; fry in batches.

Instructions:

1. **Marinate chicken:** Place chicken in a large bowl or zip-top bag. Pour buttermilk over, cover, and refrigerate for at least 4 hours or overnight.

2. **Prepare dredge:** In a shallow bowl, mix flour, paprika, garlic powder, onion powder, salt, and pepper.

3. **Dredge chicken:** Remove chicken from buttermilk, letting excess drip off. Coat thoroughly in flour mixture.

4. **Heat oil:** In a deep skillet or cast iron pan, heat about 2 inches of oil to 350°F (175°C).

5. **Fry chicken:** Fry chicken pieces in batches, turning occasionally, until golden brown and cooked through (internal temperature 165°F or 74°C), about 15-20 minutes.

6. **Drain and rest:** Transfer to a wire rack or paper towels to drain excess oil.

7. **Serve:** Enjoy hot, preferably with classic sides like mashed potatoes or coleslaw.

Traditional Casseroles for Family Dinners

Ingredients (Classic Tuna Noodle Casserole):

- 12 ounces egg noodles

- 2 cups cooked tuna, drained

- 1 can (10.5 oz) cream of mushroom soup

- 1 cup frozen peas, thawed
- 1 cup shredded cheddar cheese
- 1/2 cup milk
- 1/2 cup crushed potato chips or breadcrumbs
- Salt and pepper to taste

Cooking Time:

- Prep: 20 minutes
- Baking: 25 to 30 minutes

Cooking Tips:

- Cook noodles just until al dente to avoid mushy casserole.
- Use good-quality canned soup or homemade substitute for better flavor.
- Add crunchy topping for texture contrast.

Instructions:

1. **Preheat oven:** to 350°F (175°C).

2. **Cook noodles:** Boil noodles until al dente. Drain and set aside.

3. **Mix casserole:** In a large bowl, combine tuna, soup, peas, cheese, milk, salt, and pepper. Fold in noodles gently.

4. **Assemble:** Pour mixture into a greased baking dish.

5. **Top:** Sprinkle crushed potato chips or breadcrumbs evenly on top.

6. **Bake:** Bake uncovered for 25-30 minutes until bubbly and golden.

7. **Serve:** Let cool slightly before serving.

These hearty main dishes evoke the warmth and togetherness of family meals shared around the table. Each recipe reflects the love and care Grandma put into every meal, creating dishes that satisfy both body and soul.

Chapter 5: Side Dishes — Perfect Complements

Side dishes in Grandma's kitchen were never an afterthought. They were carefully crafted companions to the main meal, designed to balance flavors, add texture, and bring extra comfort to the table. Whether creamy, tangy, or crisp, these classic sides complete the meal and evoke memories of family gatherings filled with warmth and laughter.

In this chapter, you'll find full recipes for some of the most beloved old-fashioned side dishes—from buttery mashed potatoes to savory greens and creamy macaroni and cheese. Each recipe includes practical tips and instructions to help you bring these timeless sides to life in your own kitchen.

Creamy Mashed Potatoes and Gravy

Ingredients:

- 5 pounds russet potatoes, peeled and cut into chunks

- 1 cup whole milk or heavy cream, warmed
- 1/2 cup unsalted butter
- Salt and freshly ground black pepper to taste

For the Gravy:

- Pan drippings from roast or 3 tablespoons butter
- 3 tablespoons all-purpose flour
- 2 cups beef or chicken broth
- Salt and pepper to taste

Cooking Time:

- Potatoes boiling: 20-25 minutes
- Gravy preparation: 10-15 minutes

Cooking Tips:

- Use russet potatoes for fluffy, creamy texture.

- Don't overboil potatoes to avoid waterlogged mash.

- Warm milk and melted butter keep mashed potatoes smooth and rich.

- For silky gravy, whisk flour slowly into melted butter before adding broth.

Instructions:

1. **Cook potatoes:** Place peeled potatoes in a large pot and cover with cold water. Bring to a boil and cook until fork-tender, about 20-25 minutes. Drain well.

2. **Mash potatoes:** Return potatoes to pot or use a mixing bowl. Add warm milk and butter. Mash with a potato masher or use a ricer for extra smoothness. Season with salt and pepper.

3. **Make gravy:** In a saucepan, heat pan drippings or butter over medium heat. Whisk in flour and cook for 2 minutes until golden. Gradually whisk in broth, stirring constantly to avoid lumps. Simmer until thickened, about 5-7 minutes. Season with salt and pepper.

4. **Serve:** Spoon mashed potatoes onto plates and drizzle with hot gravy.

Southern-Style Collard Greens

Ingredients:

- 2 pounds fresh collard greens, washed, stems removed, and chopped
- 4 slices smoked bacon or ham hocks
- 1 large onion, chopped
- 3 cloves garlic, minced
- 4 cups chicken broth
- 1 tablespoon apple cider vinegar
- 1 teaspoon sugar
- Salt and pepper to taste

Cooking Time:

- Prep and sauté: 15 minutes

- Simmering: 1 to 1.5 hours

Cooking Tips:

- Remove tough stems to ensure tender greens.

- Use smoked meat for rich, smoky flavor.

- Add vinegar toward the end to brighten flavor.

- Simmer gently to prevent overcooking and bitterness.

Instructions:

1. **Cook bacon:** In a large pot, cook bacon over medium heat until crispy. Remove bacon, leaving drippings.

2. **Sauté aromatics:** Add onion and garlic to drippings, cook until softened, about 5 minutes.

3. **Add greens:** Stir in collard greens, turning to wilt slightly.

4. **Add broth and season:** Pour in chicken broth, add bacon or ham hocks back to pot. Season with salt, pepper, sugar.

5. **Simmer:** Cover and simmer on low heat for 1 to 1.5 hours, stirring occasionally until greens are tender.

6. **Finish:** Remove smoked meat, chop and stir back in or serve separately. Add a splash of vinegar just before serving.

Old-Fashioned Macaroni and Cheese

Ingredients:

- 8 ounces elbow macaroni
- 3 cups sharp cheddar cheese, shredded
- 2 cups milk
- 3 tablespoons butter
- 3 tablespoons all-purpose flour

- 1 teaspoon dry mustard powder (optional)
- Salt and pepper to taste
- 1/2 cup breadcrumbs (optional, for topping)

Cooking Time:

- Pasta cooking: 8-10 minutes
- Sauce preparation and baking: 30 minutes

Cooking Tips:

- Cook pasta al dente to avoid mushiness after baking.
- Use sharp cheddar for robust flavor.
- Dry mustard powder enhances cheesy depth.
- For a crunchy top, sprinkle breadcrumbs before baking.

Instructions:

1. **Cook pasta:** Boil macaroni according to package directions until just al dente. Drain and set aside.

2. **Make cheese sauce:** In a saucepan, melt butter over medium heat. Whisk in flour and cook for 2 minutes. Gradually whisk in milk, cook until thickened and bubbly.

3. **Add cheese:** Remove from heat, stir in shredded cheese, dry mustard, salt, and pepper until melted and smooth.

4. **Combine:** Mix cheese sauce with cooked macaroni. Pour into a greased baking dish.

5. **Top (optional):** Sprinkle breadcrumbs evenly on top.

6. **Bake:** Bake at 350°F (175°C) for 20-25 minutes until bubbly and golden on top.

7. **Serve:** Let cool slightly before serving.

Vintage Vegetable Medleys

Ingredients:

- 2 cups green beans, trimmed

- 2 cups carrots, sliced
- 1 cup pearl onions, peeled
- 1 cup mushrooms, sliced
- 3 tablespoons butter
- 1 teaspoon sugar
- Salt and pepper to taste
- Fresh parsley for garnish

Cooking Time:

- Prep and sauté: 15-20 minutes

Cooking Tips:

- Blanch vegetables briefly before sautéing to retain color and texture.
- Use fresh butter for rich flavor.

- Season lightly to let natural vegetable flavors shine.

Instructions:

1. **Blanch vegetables:** Bring a pot of salted water to boil. Blanch green beans, carrots, and pearl onions for 2-3 minutes. Drain and rinse under cold water.

2. **Sauté:** In a large skillet, melt butter over medium heat. Add mushrooms and sauté until tender, about 5 minutes.

3. **Add other vegetables:** Stir in blanched green beans, carrots, and onions. Sprinkle with sugar, salt, and pepper. Cook, stirring occasionally, for 5-7 minutes until heated through and slightly caramelized.

4. **Garnish and serve:** Sprinkle fresh parsley before serving.

Each of these side dishes perfectly complements the hearty mains, adding texture, flavor, and tradition to the meal. They invite you to savor every bite and carry forward the legacy of timeless family cooking.

Chapter 6: Preserves & Pickles — Pantry Treasures

In Grandma's kitchen, the arrival of fresh fruits and vegetables from the garden or market was only the beginning. Preserving the bounty through canning, pickling, and making jams and jellies was a treasured tradition, ensuring that the flavors of summer and fall could be enjoyed all year round. These pantry treasures not only added bursts of flavor to meals but also symbolized care, resourcefulness, and family heritage.

This chapter offers detailed recipes and instructions to help you recreate Grandma's preserves and pickles. With patience and attention, you'll learn how to transform simple ingredients into delightful condiments that bring a taste of the past to your table today.

Grandma's Sweet Strawberry Jam

Ingredients:

- 4 cups fresh strawberries, hulled and crushed

- 4 cups granulated sugar

- 1/4 cup lemon juice

Cooking Time:

- Preparation and cooking: 45 to 60 minutes

- Cooling and jarring: 1 hour

Cooking Tips:

- Use ripe, fragrant strawberries for the best flavor.

- Sterilize jars and lids to ensure safe preservation.

- Stir frequently to prevent sticking and burning.

- Test for gel by placing a small spoonful on a cold plate — it should wrinkle when pushed.

Instructions:

1. **Prepare jars:** Sterilize canning jars and lids by boiling them in water for 10 minutes. Keep warm until ready to fill.

2. **Crush berries:** In a large pot, crush strawberries using a potato masher or fork.

3. **Add sugar and lemon juice:** Stir in sugar and lemon juice. Let the mixture sit for 10 minutes to dissolve sugar.

4. **Cook jam:** Bring mixture to a boil over medium-high heat, stirring constantly. Boil hard for 15-20 minutes or until thickened and gel point is reached.

5. **Fill jars:** Remove from heat and ladle hot jam into sterilized jars, leaving 1/4-inch headspace. Wipe rims clean.

6. **Seal:** Place lids on jars and screw on bands until fingertip tight.

7. **Process:** Boil jars in a water bath for 10 minutes to seal. Remove and cool completely.

8. **Store:** Label and store in a cool, dark place. Refrigerate after opening.

Classic Bread and Butter Pickles

Ingredients:

- 6 cups thinly sliced cucumbers
- 2 cups thinly sliced onions
- 1/4 cup salt
- 2 cups white vinegar
- 1 1/2 cups granulated sugar
- 1 tablespoon mustard seeds
- 1 teaspoon turmeric
- 1 teaspoon celery seeds

Cooking Time:

- Preparation and soaking: 2 hours
- Cooking: 10 to 15 minutes

Cooking Tips:

- Use firm, fresh cucumbers for crisp pickles.

- Soak cucumber and onions in salt to draw out excess moisture.

- Sterilize jars for safe storage.

Instructions:

1. **Prepare vegetables:** Combine cucumbers, onions, and salt in a large bowl. Toss well and let sit for 2 hours, stirring occasionally. Drain and rinse.

2. **Make brine:** In a large pot, combine vinegar, sugar, mustard seeds, turmeric, and celery seeds. Bring to a boil, stirring to dissolve sugar.

3. **Cook pickles:** Add cucumber and onion mixture to the brine. Cook for 10-15 minutes until vegetables are tender but still crisp.

4. **Pack jars:** Ladle hot pickles into sterilized jars, leaving 1/2 inch headspace.

5. **Seal:** Wipe rims, place lids, and tighten bands.

6. **Process:** Boil jars in water bath for 10 minutes. Remove and cool.

7. **Store:** Label and store in a cool, dark place. Refrigerate after opening.

Homemade Apple Butter and Fruit Preserves

Ingredients for Apple Butter:

- 5 pounds apples, peeled, cored, and chopped
- 2 cups granulated sugar
- 2 teaspoons ground cinnamon
- 1/2 teaspoon ground cloves
- 1/4 teaspoon salt
- 1 tablespoon lemon juice

Cooking Time:

- Preparation and slow cooking: 3 to 4 hours

Cooking Tips:

- Use a mix of sweet and tart apples for balanced flavor.
- Stir frequently to prevent sticking and burning.
- Cook slowly until the mixture is thick and spreadable.

Instructions:

1. **Prepare apples:** Place chopped apples in a large pot with lemon juice and a splash of water.
2. **Cook apples:** Simmer on low heat, stirring occasionally, until apples are soft, about 1 hour.
3. **Mash and season:** Use a potato masher or immersion blender to puree apples. Add sugar, cinnamon, cloves, and salt.
4. **Cook down:** Continue to cook on low heat, stirring frequently, until mixture is thick and dark brown, about 2-3

hours.

5. **Jar and store:** Pour hot apple butter into sterilized jars, seal, and process in boiling water bath for 10 minutes. Cool and store.

Pickled Vegetables for Every Season

Ingredients:

- Assorted vegetables (carrots, cauliflower, green beans, peppers)
- 4 cups white vinegar
- 4 cups water
- 1/4 cup sugar
- 2 tablespoons salt
- 1 tablespoon mustard seeds

- 1 tablespoon dill seeds

- 4 garlic cloves, peeled

Cooking Time:

- Preparation and packing: 30 minutes

- Pickling: 24 hours to several weeks

Cooking Tips:

- Cut vegetables into uniform sizes for even pickling.

- Sterilize jars and lids before use.

- Let pickles develop flavor in refrigerator for best results.

Instructions:

1. **Prepare vegetables:** Wash and cut vegetables into bite-sized pieces.

2. **Sterilize jars:** Clean jars and lids by boiling for 10 minutes.

3. **Make brine:** In a pot, combine vinegar, water, sugar, salt, mustard seeds, dill seeds, and garlic. Bring to a boil.

4. **Pack jars:** Tightly pack vegetables into sterilized jars.

5. **Add brine:** Pour hot brine over vegetables, leaving 1/2 inch headspace.

6. **Seal jars:** Place lids and bands on jars.

7. **Cool and store:** Let jars cool to room temperature, then refrigerate. Pickles develop flavor after at least 24 hours; best after 1-2 weeks.

Chapter 7: Desserts & Sweet Treats — Sweet Memories from Grandma's Kitchen

Desserts in Grandma's kitchen were the grand finale, a celebration of simple pleasures and heartfelt traditions. These sweet treats were often made from scratch with ingredients readily available, yet they carried a richness of flavor and a warmth of nostalgia that no store-bought dessert could match. From warm apple crisps bubbling out of the oven to soft sugar cookies and rich chocolate cakes, these recipes invite you to recreate the joy of those special moments shared around the family table.

In this chapter, you'll find detailed recipes with clear instructions and tips to help you bake classic desserts that have been treasured through generations. Whether you're baking for a holiday, a family gathering, or just to satisfy a sweet craving, these old-fashioned treats bring comfort and happiness in every bite.

Old-Fashioned Apple Crisp

Ingredients:

- 6 cups peeled and sliced tart apples (such as Granny Smith)
- 1 tablespoon lemon juice
- 3/4 cup granulated sugar
- 1 teaspoon ground cinnamon
- 1/2 teaspoon ground nutmeg

Topping:

- 1 cup all-purpose flour
- 1 cup rolled oats
- 3/4 cup packed brown sugar
- 1/2 cup cold unsalted butter, diced
- 1/2 teaspoon salt

Cooking Time:

- Prep: 20 minutes

- Baking: 40-45 minutes

Cooking Tips:

- Use tart apples for balanced sweetness and texture.

- Cut butter into topping until mixture resembles coarse crumbs.

- Bake until topping is golden and apples are tender but not mushy.

Instructions:

1. **Preheat oven:** to 350°F (175°C).

2. **Prepare apples:** Toss sliced apples with lemon juice, sugar, cinnamon, and nutmeg. Spread evenly in a greased 9x13-inch baking dish.

3. **Make topping:** In a bowl, combine flour, oats, brown sugar, and salt. Cut in cold butter using a pastry cutter or fingers until mixture resembles coarse crumbs.

4. **Assemble:** Sprinkle topping evenly over apples.

5. **Bake:** Bake for 40-45 minutes until topping is golden brown and apples are bubbly.

6. **Serve:** Best served warm, often with a scoop of vanilla ice cream or whipped cream.

Chocolate Sheet Cake with Fudge Frosting

Ingredients for Cake:

- 2 cups all-purpose flour

- 2 cups granulated sugar

- 1/2 teaspoon salt

- 1/4 cup unsweetened cocoa powder

- 1 cup unsalted butter

- 1 cup water

- 1/2 cup buttermilk
- 2 large eggs
- 1 teaspoon baking soda
- 1 teaspoon vanilla extract

Ingredients for Fudge Frosting:

- 1/2 cup unsalted butter
- 1/4 cup unsweetened cocoa powder
- 6 tablespoons milk
- 1 teaspoon vanilla extract
- 3 1/2 cups powdered sugar

Cooking Time:

- Cake prep and baking: 30 minutes
- Frosting preparation: 10 minutes

Cooking Tips:

- Use unsweetened cocoa for rich chocolate flavor.
- Beat eggs and buttermilk thoroughly for moist cake.
- Frost while cake is still warm for easy spreading and absorption.

Instructions:

1. **Preheat oven:** to 350°F (175°C). Grease and flour a 13x9-inch baking pan.

2. **Make cake batter:** In a large bowl, combine flour, sugar, salt, and cocoa powder. In a saucepan, bring butter and water to a boil. Pour hot mixture into dry ingredients and mix well.

3. **Add eggs and buttermilk:** Beat in eggs, baking soda (dissolved in buttermilk), and vanilla extract until smooth.

4. **Bake:** Pour batter into prepared pan. Bake 30-35 minutes or until a toothpick inserted in center comes out clean.

5. **Prepare frosting:** In a saucepan, melt butter. Stir in cocoa powder and milk, bring to a boil. Remove from heat, add

vanilla and powdered sugar, and beat until smooth.

6. **Frost cake:** Pour frosting over warm cake, spreading evenly.

7. **Cool and serve:** Let cake cool before cutting.

Classic Rice Pudding and Custards

Ingredients for Rice Pudding:

- 1/2 cup long-grain white rice
- 4 cups whole milk
- 3/4 cup granulated sugar
- 1/4 teaspoon salt
- 1 teaspoon vanilla extract
- Ground cinnamon or nutmeg for garnish

Cooking Time:

- Prep and simmering: 50-60 minutes

Cooking Tips:

- Stir frequently to prevent rice from sticking.
- Use whole milk for creamy texture.
- Let pudding cool slightly to thicken further.

Instructions:

1. **Combine ingredients:** In a heavy saucepan, combine rice, milk, sugar, and salt.

2. **Cook:** Bring to a gentle simmer over medium heat, stirring frequently. Reduce heat to low and simmer uncovered for 45-50 minutes or until rice is tender and mixture thickens.

3. **Finish:** Remove from heat, stir in vanilla.

4. **Serve:** Spoon into bowls, sprinkle with cinnamon or nutmeg. Serve warm or chilled.

Grandma's Famous Sugar Cookies

Ingredients:

- 2 3/4 cups all-purpose flour
- 1 teaspoon baking soda
- 1/2 teaspoon baking powder
- 1 cup unsalted butter, softened
- 1 1/2 cups granulated sugar
- 1 egg
- 1 teaspoon vanilla extract
- 1/2 teaspoon salt

Cooking Time:

- Prep and chilling: 1 hour
- Baking: 8-10 minutes

Cooking Tips:

- Chill dough before rolling to prevent spreading.

- Roll dough evenly for uniform cookies.

- Don't overbake; cookies should be just set and lightly golden at edges.

Instructions:

1. **Preheat oven:** to 375°F (190°C).

2. **Mix dry ingredients:** In a bowl, whisk flour, baking soda, baking powder, and salt.

3. **Cream butter and sugar:** In a separate bowl, beat butter and sugar until fluffy.

4. **Add egg and vanilla:** Beat in egg and vanilla extract.

5. **Combine:** Gradually add flour mixture to butter mixture until combined.

6. **Chill dough:** Wrap dough and chill for at least 1 hour.

7. **Roll and cut:** Roll out dough on floured surface to 1/4 inch thickness. Cut into shapes with cookie cutters.

8. **Bake:** Place cookies on greased baking sheet. Bake 8-10 minutes until edges are lightly golden.

9. **Cool:** Let cool on wire racks before decorating or serving.

Chapter 8: Holiday & Special Occasion Recipes

Holidays and special occasions in Grandma's kitchen were times of joy, tradition, and togetherness. These recipes capture the spirit of celebration, featuring dishes that were lovingly prepared to mark important moments with family and friends. From classic Thanksgiving sides to festive cookies and cakes, these dishes are filled with flavors that evoke warmth and nostalgia.

In this chapter, you'll discover detailed recipes designed to help you recreate those cherished holiday meals and treats, complete with tips for preparation and presentation that will make any occasion feel truly special.

Traditional Thanksgiving Favorites

Roast Turkey with Herb Butter

Ingredients:

- 1 whole turkey (12-14 pounds)

- 1 cup unsalted butter, softened

- 4 cloves garlic, minced

- 2 tablespoons fresh rosemary, chopped

- 2 tablespoons fresh thyme, chopped

- Salt and pepper to taste

- 1 onion, quartered

- 2 carrots, chopped

- 2 celery stalks, chopped

- 2 cups chicken broth

Cooking Time:

- Preparation: 30 minutes

- Roasting: 3 to 4 hours

Tips:

- Let turkey come to room temperature before roasting.

- Use a meat thermometer to ensure perfect doneness (165°F internal temperature).

- Baste turkey periodically with pan juices for moist, flavorful meat.

Instructions:

1. Preheat oven to 325°F (165°C).

2. In a bowl, combine softened butter, garlic, rosemary, thyme, salt, and pepper.

3. Pat turkey dry and loosen skin over breast carefully. Spread herb butter under skin and over entire turkey.

4. Stuff cavity with onion, carrots, and celery. Place turkey on roasting rack in a roasting pan.

5. Pour chicken broth into pan. Roast turkey, basting every 30 minutes, until internal temperature reaches 165°F.

6. Let rest for 20 minutes before carving.

Classic Christmas Cookies and Treats

Gingerbread Cookies

Ingredients:

- 3 cups all-purpose flour
- 3/4 cup brown sugar
- 1 tablespoon ground ginger
- 2 teaspoons ground cinnamon
- 1/2 teaspoon ground cloves
- 1/2 teaspoon baking soda
- 1/4 teaspoon salt
- 3/4 cup unsalted butter, softened
- 3/4 cup molasses
- 1 egg

Cooking Time:

- Prep: 20 minutes

- Baking: 8-10 minutes

Tips:

- Chill dough to make rolling and cutting easier.

- Use cookie cutters to create festive shapes.

- Decorate with icing or sprinkles once cooled.

Instructions:

1. Whisk flour, sugar, ginger, cinnamon, cloves, baking soda, and salt.

2. In a separate bowl, beat butter, molasses, and egg until smooth.

3. Gradually add dry ingredients to wet, mixing well.

4. Chill dough for at least 1 hour.

5. Roll dough to 1/4 inch thickness; cut shapes and place on baking sheet.

6. Bake at 350°F (175°C) for 8-10 minutes. Cool on wire racks before decorating.

Heirloom Recipes for Family Gatherings

Classic Deviled Eggs

Ingredients:

- 12 large eggs
- 1/2 cup mayonnaise
- 2 teaspoons Dijon mustard
- 1 teaspoon white vinegar
- Salt and pepper to taste
- Paprika for garnish

Cooking Time:

- Boiling eggs: 15 minutes

- Preparation: 15 minutes

Tips:

- Use older eggs for easier peeling.

- Chill eggs before peeling.

- Mix filling until smooth but not runny.

Instructions:

1. Place eggs in a pot and cover with water. Bring to a boil and cook for 12 minutes.

2. Transfer eggs to ice water and cool completely. Peel and halve lengthwise.

3. Remove yolks and mash with mayonnaise, mustard, vinegar, salt, and pepper.

4. Spoon or pipe yolk mixture back into whites.

5. Sprinkle with paprika before serving.

Festive Breads and Cakes

Holiday Fruitcake

Ingredients:

- 2 cups mixed dried fruit (raisins, cherries, apricots)
- 1 cup chopped nuts (walnuts, pecans)
- 1 cup dark brown sugar
- 1 cup unsalted butter
- 4 large eggs
- 2 cups all-purpose flour
- 1 teaspoon baking powder
- 1/2 teaspoon salt
- 1/2 cup orange juice

- 1 teaspoon vanilla extract
- 1 teaspoon ground cinnamon

Cooking Time:

- Preparation: 30 minutes
- Baking: 1 1/2 to 2 hours

Tips:

- Soak dried fruits overnight in orange juice for moist cake.
- Use a loaf pan lined with parchment for easy removal.
- Wrap cake in cloth soaked in brandy after baking for richer flavor (optional).

Instructions:

1. Preheat oven to 300°F (150°C). Grease and line a loaf pan.
2. Cream butter and sugar until fluffy. Add eggs one at a time.

3. Mix flour, baking powder, salt, cinnamon in a separate bowl.

4. Gradually add dry ingredients to wet mixture, alternating with orange juice and vanilla.

5. Fold in soaked dried fruits and nuts.

6. Pour batter into pan and bake 1.5 to 2 hours until a toothpick comes out clean.

7. Cool completely before slicing.

Chapter 9: Kitchen Tips & Time-Tested Tricks

Grandma's kitchen was filled with more than just recipes—it was a treasure trove of wisdom, practical tips, and clever tricks honed over years of cooking. These time-tested techniques helped make cooking easier, more efficient, and more enjoyable, especially in a time before modern conveniences and gadgets. In this chapter, you'll discover invaluable advice passed down through generations to elevate your cooking and bring the same warmth and success to your kitchen that Grandma's did.

How to Make Homemade Stock and Broth

Homemade stock is the foundation of countless recipes, providing rich flavor and depth to soups, stews, sauces, and more. Grandma always said that a good stock was worth its weight in gold—and making your own is simpler than you might think.

Tips for making stock:

- Use leftover bones from chicken, beef, or pork along with vegetable scraps like onion skins, carrot peels, and celery ends.

- Simmer gently for several hours (3-6 hours for chicken, up to 12 for beef) to extract maximum flavor without cloudiness.

- Avoid boiling vigorously, which can make stock cloudy and bitter.

- Skim off foam and impurities regularly for a clear broth.

- Cool quickly and store in airtight containers; homemade stock freezes well for months.

Preserving Freshness: Freezing and Canning Basics

Before refrigeration was widespread, freezing and canning were essential for preserving seasonal bounty. Grandma mastered both, using simple methods that keep food fresh and safe.

Freezing tips:

- Blanch vegetables before freezing to preserve color, texture, and nutrients.

- Freeze in portion-sized containers or bags for convenience.

- Label everything with date and contents to avoid confusion later.

Canning tips:

- Always sterilize jars and lids before use.

- Follow trusted recipes closely, especially for acidity and processing times, to prevent spoilage.

- Use a water bath canner for high-acid foods like jams and pickles; use a pressure canner for low-acid foods like meats and vegetables.

- Check seals before storage—sealed lids should not flex when pressed.

Secret Ingredient Swaps and Enhancements

Sometimes Grandma's magic came from small tweaks—adding a pinch of something special to elevate a dish.

- **Add a splash of vinegar or lemon juice:** Brightens flavors in soups, stews, and greens.
- **A spoonful of sour cream or yogurt:** Adds creaminess and tang to sauces and dressings.
- **Use browned butter:** Deepens flavor in baked goods and vegetables.
- **Season with fresh herbs at the end:** Preserves their bright, fresh flavor.
- **A dash of smoked paprika or cayenne:** Adds warmth and complexity without overwhelming.

Tools and Techniques Grandma Swore By

Grandma didn't have fancy kitchen gadgets, but she knew how to get great results with what she had.

- **Cast iron skillets:** For even heat and perfect searing, a well-seasoned cast iron pan was indispensable.

- **Wooden spoons:** Gentle on cookware and perfect for stirring thick batters and sauces.

- **Sharp knives:** Essential for safe, efficient prep; Grandma sharpened hers regularly.

- **Rolling pins:** For making perfect pie crusts and pastries.

- **Slow cookers or Dutch ovens:** For hands-off, slow-simmered dishes full of flavor and tenderness.

Chapter 10: Stories & Memories from Grandma's Kitchen

Grandma's kitchen was more than just a place to prepare food—it was the heart of the home, where stories were told, laughter echoed, and memories were woven into every meal. The recipes in this book are rooted not only in ingredients and techniques but also in the rich traditions and cherished moments that made cooking with Grandma so special.

In this chapter, we celebrate those stories and memories that bring life to the dishes and remind us why food is so much more than sustenance. These tales offer insight into the history behind the recipes and the love that infused every bite.

Cherished Family Traditions

Many of Grandma's recipes were tied to specific occasions—Sunday dinners, holiday celebrations, or simple weekday meals that brought the family together. Each dish was a thread in the fabric of family life, passed down and adapted over time but always reminding everyone of their roots.

For example, Sunday pot roast wasn't just a meal—it was the centerpiece of a day filled with family stories, games, and rest. The apple crisp was a dessert that brought comfort after chilly autumn days, often enjoyed by the fireplace with everyone gathered around.

Grandma's tradition of making preserves every summer was both practical and celebratory—a way to capture the fleeting abundance of the season and share it throughout the year. These preserved jars symbolized care and continuity, gifts of flavor and love passed from one generation to the next.

The History Behind Our Favorite Recipes

Many recipes have origins that go back generations, sometimes tracing to faraway places and times. The cornbread recipe, for instance, reflects the influence of Southern cooking traditions, where cornmeal was a staple. The chicken and dumplings recipe is rooted in early American rural kitchens, where stretching simple ingredients into filling dishes was essential.

Understanding these histories adds depth to the cooking experience. It connects us to the hardships and celebrations of those who came before, honoring their resilience and creativity. It also highlights the cultural influences that shaped family kitchens, making every recipe a story waiting to be told.

Letters and Notes from Grandma's Recipe Box

In Grandma's worn recipe box, there were not just recipes but also handwritten notes, scraps of paper with ingredient substitutions, and reminders about cooking times. These little annotations speak volumes about the personal nature of cooking—how it's shaped by experimentation, adaptation, and love.

One note might suggest adding a pinch of nutmeg to the apple pie, while another reminds to "slow cook stew low and slow." These insights remind us that recipes are living documents, evolving with each cook's touch.

Sharing these notes here is a tribute to that spirit, encouraging you to make these recipes your own, adding your voice to the ongoing story.

Reflections on the Art of Cooking with Love

Grandma always said the secret ingredient was love—not just in the romantic sense but in the care and attention you put into every step. Cooking wasn't a chore; it was a way to nurture, to celebrate, and to connect.

This mindset transforms food from mere fuel into a source of comfort and joy. When you cook with love, even the simplest meal becomes meaningful, creating bonds that linger long after the plates are cleared.

Remembering this is the true gift of Grandma's kitchen. It teaches us to slow down, be present, and appreciate the process as much as the product.

Conclusion

As we come to the close of *Timeless Grandma Old Fashion Cookbook: Heirloom Flavors from the Heart of the Kitchen*, it's clear that this book is far more than a collection of recipes. It is a journey—a journey through time, through family traditions, and through the simple, powerful act of sharing food made with love. The pages you have turned are filled with dishes that connect us to our past and inspire us to bring that same warmth into our present and future kitchens.

Grandma's cooking was never just about nourishment. It was about community, care, and creating a space where love was tasted as much as it was felt. Each recipe is a reflection of her hands, her heart, and her home. They carry with them the stories of countless meals shared, of celebrations big and small, and of everyday moments made special by the food on the table.

In a world that often moves too fast, where convenience sometimes overshadows tradition, the lessons found here invite us to slow down and rediscover the value of cooking with intention. To measure ingredients not just with cups and spoons, but with patience, kindness, and a genuine desire to nurture those we care about.

The timeless recipes in this book remind us that good food is accessible to everyone, made from simple, wholesome ingredients that have sustained families for generations. Whether it's the golden biscuits that start a Southern breakfast, the hearty stews that warm the coldest nights, or the sweet apple crisp that ends a meal with a sigh of contentment, these dishes are built on fundamentals—honesty, simplicity, and love.

Beyond the food itself, you have glimpsed the wisdom and practicality that made Grandma's kitchen a place of magic. The tips, tricks, and stories included throughout the chapters are a testament to a way of life where resourcefulness and care transformed ordinary ingredients into something extraordinary. From making your own stock to preserving the harvest, these skills connect us to a heritage that is rich, rewarding, and deeply human.

As you return to your own kitchen, I encourage you to take these recipes and make them your own. Add your voice to the ongoing story by adapting flavors to suit your family, by sharing meals with friends, and by creating new memories that will one day become cherished traditions. Don't be afraid to experiment or to slow the pace when needed; cooking is as much about the journey as it is about the destination.

Remember that the true secret to Grandma's kitchen isn't found in the ingredients or techniques alone—it is found in the intention behind each dish. It is the desire to provide comfort, to celebrate togetherness, and to pass on something meaningful from one generation to the next. When you cook with love, the simplest meal can become a feast of connection.

This book is your invitation to embrace that spirit. To fill your kitchen with warmth, with laughter, and with the rich aromas of meals that have stood the test of time. To gather your loved ones around the table and share not just food, but stories, traditions, and moments that linger long after the last bite.

In closing, I want to leave you with this thought: Every recipe you prepare, every meal you share, is part of a larger legacy. It is the continuation of a story written by those who came before us and carried forward by those who will come after. By cooking these heirloom flavors, you honor that legacy and keep it alive in your own unique way.

So here's to Grandma's kitchen—the heart of the home, the keeper of stories, and the source of timeless flavors. May your cooking be filled with joy, your table with abundance, and your home with love.

Thank you for joining this journey through the flavors and memories of a kitchen that has fed generations. May these recipes nourish your body, inspire your heart, and bring your family closer, one delicious meal at a time.

Printed in Dunstable, United Kingdom